Erasing bodies

Poems for the living...

Ipsita Banerjee

BookLeaf Publishing

India | USA | UK

Made with ❤ on the BookLeaf Publishing Platform
www.bookleafpub.in
www.bookleafpub.com

To the beginning, Baba, when you were always
there.

Acknowledgements

My daughters, Isha and Amisha, have been my solid support for all the times when I was down and the times when I was very down. So yes, this goes out to them, along with our dogs, Hector and Loki, for their boundless energy. These are my people; they are my succour, my strength. Without them, I could not have made it this far.

Thanks to all the people at BookLeaf Publishing (especially Farida, Tahira and Roosha, my editor), who have been immensely patient with me and my endless questions and who have given me an opportunity to take this book to reality.

A shout-out to my husband, Amitesh, for his support and for reminding me of the '*joie de verve*' I was missing in my life.

And to you, gentle reader, who has this book in your hands, I hope some of my poetry resonates with you.

Preface

This book was actually named during one of those long and endless days of the COVID lockdown. Scrolling through my phone, as we all did then, I came across yet another Instagram (or whatever) post that told me that matching my date of birth with my month of birth and my year of birth would tell me the name of the book I should write… (yes, the world was pseudo-normal for a while!). And that's how I got the name for my book, which stuck with me. Actually, it was 'erasing bodies in a crisis'. But there are no crises here. Not now, anyway. You will see what I mean, I hope, by the time you get to the end of this book.

Next, I was incorrect when I said there was no crisis. There have been issues in the family. And illnesses that we all have been coping with. Several things, big and small. So the idea of writing this book was to bring everything to a standstill, to a place where we erase the bodies of all that is lost. And raise the bodies of all that we have but do not necessarily want. We all have the weight of bodies to carry as we move through life; not just the bodies of our loved ones, our thoughts, our longings, our mistakes, but also of our past loves, our earlier lives. They never go away and live with us for as long as we do. Do we ever get what we want? And when we do, are we ever content?

Yet, this book is also about hope, about looking ahead, getting past all the bodies we carry of all that is gone. No matter the cost, no matter what came before.

This reminds me of a beautiful poem by Kenyatta Rogers, which goes like this:

Ars Poetica (after Amiri Baraka and Stefani Gomez)
"Poems are bullshit unless they are broken
like a horse, like a dog kicked in the ribs,
Like your favorite toy that's missing an arm.

Love can make you feel used.
I want the poem that limps back to me.
Poems should hurt like love,
like ice water on your teeth
like a massage to smooth out a cramped muscle.

Give me the poem that's like leather.
Give me the poem that smells like gasoline.
I want a poem that is a warning,
a poem that makes me check to see

if I left the shotgun by the door,
a poem that's a runny nose, a sneeze, a poem
that's the moment the sky turns green."

So do my poems limp back to anyone? That, dear
Reader, is for you to decide.

Lost

I never talked about God with my mother
I did not tell her a lot of things
like how I struggle to sleep, or laugh,
or go through yet another day.
I tell no one that I am sad,
how, when I let my soul wander
it goes away. I do not even talk
about how I don't care anymore
if it returns. I used to tell my father
about myriad thoughts and things...
But I let him wander; sometimes I feel
my soul just walks with him.

There's a dungeon in my head,
where I have chained myself
to walls slimy with the sweat
of lives long gone, where the light retreats
through a barred window, where darkness
saunters in, whispering sweet nothings,
whistling in my head. Come, sit with me
for a while, I will offer you a meal
made lovingly with hands
that pull apart the flesh
digging into bones and meat, trying to wash
off the blood you never want to see.

'Too late,' a voice whispers to me,
'she is gone now, the one
you wished to please, leaving only scraps
of the darkness you have culled
with these bare, bloodied hands,
and a soul that cannot bear to be free.'

The five senses

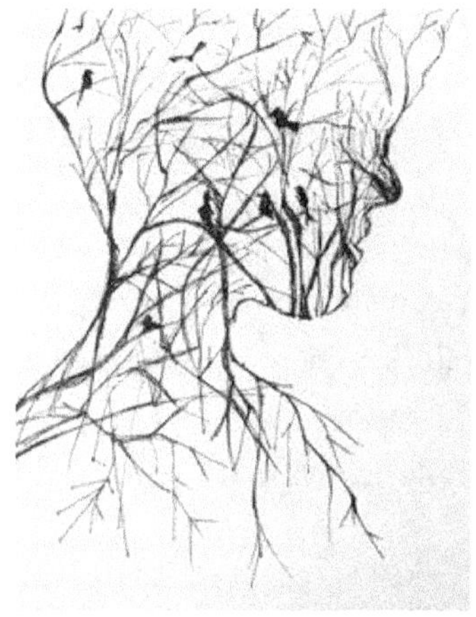

Winter came early this year.
Across the city, the smell of smoke and
naphthalene
as fires are lit, sweaters shake themselves out of
trunks.
The moon swims among the clouds as I walk the
empty streets,
the pavement dwellers are gone; they huddle
behind doors
deep inside the narrow streets where moonlight
dares not reach;
those corners which light has abandoned even
during the day.

There is a stench here, the stench of beasts
pretending to be human,
the stench of old money passed around from hand
to hand,
the stench of a sleeper-class train that clings to
your shirt.

I look up at you and you look away,
my words fall flat; there are no answers anymore,
are there?
As I keep walking, my roads wind and twist and
turn
sometimes I see you, sometimes I only think I
do...
your footsteps go away and return to fade into the
night
I hear the voices in my head, the voices that are
lost:
the solemn sound of the 9 AM siren on a Sunday,
the rippling sound of the stones you skipped upon
the lake,
your boisterous laugh as you called out my name,
for no reason, you said, only because you liked to.

Yes, I have tasted failure; its bitterness is rough,
cutting at the mouth with the metallic tinge of
blood
I have reached for your hand into the darkness

and have found yours, reaching out to me.
I have lain my head upon your shoulder and cried
your hands have soothed the fever from my brow,
I even have gardenias growing in the garden
for the five senses I have mastered, they think you
walk with me;
it is my heart that is the lonely traitor,
only my heart knows the truth.

One day I will cry

One day I will cry. And I will cry a river
cascading over landscapes unknown
thundering over rocks and stones
carving a path of its very own.

And when the tears finally meet the sea,
it will be on a widened estuary
peaceful and calm, no deltas for me
no dredging on the edge to carry.

No second look, no longing thought,
no tributaries running hither and to.
I will open my tidal mouth wide and full,
when I have to go, I will just go.

Oh, beautiful world with all its heartache
lend me some more, so I find reprieve
one day I will cry, I am certain I will,
and you will smile and say, *it's okay to grieve.*

The pyre

I crawled into the pyre with you
the day I committed you to flames,
is it any surprise, then, that heat,
is something I only know by name?

I walked with you by your side
when each broken step was cursed
can you blame me, then, if I
know not which footprint was yours?

I was there to try to share your pain
when each breath you took was a vice
through the dark, I hear your voice call out
can you say, then, I heed not your voice?

I was silent when they took you away,
I held my peace when they said I was wrong
can you hold it, then, against me,
when I say, I live, only off your love?

Cages

There was this little bird I killed.
I did not wring its neck, but
that blue budgie died by my hand
as I opened the gate of the cage,
a crow pounced on it all at once
ripped it to shreds while I cried,
struck with horror. I was a toddler
but I already hated the cage.

I hated the zoo, too, especially the tigers
stuck in cells with barely space to pace
and stupid humans jeering them along,
their lives open to scrutiny, dependent
and confined. Animals belong in the wild.
just as flowers belong on trees. When
I told my father, he smiled and ruffled my hair,
'But cages have their uses too, you'll see.'

I've been trying to list the uses
for the caged birds gazing at the trees
for the flowers drying on the altar
for the animals wailing to be freed.
And I have failed. But then I looked
around me, heard the rattling
of the chains and I thought, aren't we all
living in cages, made by society?

I did not want to kill that budgie
I only wished to set it free.
But how many of us are not in chains?
Some cages you cannot see.

The dead

The sun sets early in this place
and does not return for days
from across the horizon
come the wistful murmurs
in voices of loved ones, long dead.

There are no human footprints
to dispel the stillness with noise
no questions that need to be answered
no annoyance of a phone screeching,
the living, at last, have been silenced.

Come, sit by my side if you can find me
restless in the darkening void
all that is good, all that is glowing
are hidden within your hands,
hands that hold mine, fists unclenched.

Together we will celebrate those lives
the ones who died but walk by our side
the footsteps receding only to return
the voices softening only to resonate
the ones who we cannot let depart.

No coming back, the wise ones say.

Yet you and I, we know the dead wait.
A hand paused on the door,
a fragrance that cannot be explained...
To smile and reminisce, lest we forget.

The last time

If my grief has lost its bite,
what will I write about? Will my words
have guts and grit, will they make you cry?
I got the colour palette mixed up,
the hues lost in words I never
wanted to have to say. I never did find
the knives that were pulled out
of my stomach when you lied.

Wishing is all I do, and I do it well.
I am not a poet enough to make you feel
the joy of being and belonging,
to make you taste the salt-sea flavour
of friendship that has endured
over years. Nor can I make you see
the moonlight as it curves
into branches as I speak.

There will always be others,
they will also go where lovers go
when they are gone, deep into shadows
of the past: What if I never write again?
What if this is my very last poem?
What if my loss never returns
and I turn away? What then,
would you lie to me again?

Moving on

I want to climb on top of that flag pole
And fling myself on the ground below
My body spattering among parked cars,
my blood mixing in the rain-drenched street.
Sometimes that is all I want, to embrace
the end, to accept that this IS the end, although
it is nothing like I craved or imagined my life
to be. I used to think myself a fighter, yet
now I find myself giving up. All too easily,
the threads that bind me shredding away
one by one, as they did when you lay dying
one ragged breath at a time. You loved to say
'it is not the end of the world.' Then why
does it feel like it is? I must be one of the few
who think in sepia tones of the past, who see
fire as freedom. There is no fire stronger
than the one that swallowed you, nothing
that burns as much, ashes cooled by mid-summer
rain. This is me moving on, alternating
between grief and release in morbid monologues.
I hope it rains tonight; I will howl
at the moon I will not see, I will rage
at the moon I know is there. And I will feel.
I will feel as though I'm talking to you.

Missing

We wrest from the Earth what we cannot
possibly return, the rocks, the Rhododendron,
claiming it to be our own; a sad little goat
tied to a pole, bleating for a mother, a ghost
long slaughtered. Any stretch of land, we strip
and tar and pave, get a shout-out for this
impudent achievement. People throng
to visit this strange new vista, not caring
about the footprints left ever after.

In the milliseconds and minutes of my life
gone past, when I no longer am the flesh
of a life lost: I think of you. Only you
as another year rolls by, full of fear,
the terror of a thousand milestones cast
away. My children & my children's
children will inherit those silver linings
upon the clouds, the sudden splash of rain
that I still feel I cannot return.
Of course there's the climbing ivy
and orchids, running wild, as you trim
with shears that cut at the grain.

Are you still here, watching over me?
Is that your hand I feel in mine?
And yet and yet and yet, another year goes by
the undertow of the current resounds
to the little girl that reigns in me, the
duck we had repeats itself, quack
quack-quack, searching for you
even when you did not belong.
Did you ever not belong? I feel that now
between the mountains and the wilderness
real life that flickers, maybe, now, I am free?
Of the fluttering diastole and systole
in my heart and lungs and thumbs, numb.
Numb from the cries, the edifices of loss, lies,
as the colours turn to spring, we shade our eyes.

Oranges and yellows and red, the colours you
love spill from my mouth: unaccountable
in multiple memories, and a sense
of a sickness that does not die.
There is where we go, you and I.

For the living

You may think I'm morbid but every time
I watch the flames of the pyre, it feels
as though the fire reclaims its own.
In the end we are all ash, returning to the earth
from whence we were born. In my mind
I see you, standing by another pyre
quite unlike this. I see you turn your face
away from the smoke, the distinct smell
of burning flesh as a breeze ripples
across the river and you blink
away a tear and turn to me and say,
'Life is for the living, never forget.'

What then, do we do with the dead?
The ones that live within us, the fingers
that curl towards ours and delve
into our sleep? Where do we display
the urns that contain memories of love
and laughter? Where do we place the bouquets
of freshly cut tears? And how do we scatter
the ashes when they are interred in our bones?
I know you walk with me, surely, as
the moon, the sun, the stars. And I live
like you'd want me to, never once forgetting
that life is for the living: it always was.

Birthdays

I never did understand the point
of a birthday, for it brings with it
feelings of dread, will they try
to surprise me, or will they find
the wishes I left unsaid?
There could be better days, I guess,
to celebrate a life, a birth,
the day I gave up on giving up, for one,
or the day I went away into the night
and found the fireflies to my delight.
There could be many other days, why just one?
Days spent trudging on fields of ice,
days when I have walked alone
no hand to left or right
and come out stronger, reborn.
There could be light without flames,
there could be joy in the darkness
like a moment of warmth you think is fire
a gentle touch that is luminous
but never will be more than that.

Thoughts

In this oasis, the eucalyptus trees
are petrifying to stone. The stumps remain,
exposed to wind and rain, a reminder
of that which was. Has been.
And is gone. Once, far away from here,
we ran and played near trees like these.
(They eat the soil, or so they say...)
Mangoes graced and lit the garden,
are they still there? I'd like to think so, yes.

There are so many lives than these,
my body holds its shape. More or less.
I think of the deaths I must have died:
one day the earth fell away and they came
to wash my hands and feet and turn
my body this way and that
squeezing my limbs into clothes
that I never otherwise would wear.
(Not noticing how I'd eat their soil, their air!)

How people said, '_____ loved this, or that...'
without a care of who I really was. Or thought.
I was precious for that little while,
made me laugh, the gurgle unheard (of course),
and when I returned, the world had changed. Yet

the same night-blossoms littered, the breeze
rustled the leaves on the trees. Once again,
I live. But, then, again, you do not know me.
(Did they not say, I will eat into your soul.)

Ruin

The pool blazes in the sunlight
lit by fires that have no kindling
the smell of smoke that is not there
abrading my skin, have I touched a nerve?
The dogs follow me into the pool
The heat is unbearable but chills
Nothing moves, even the birds are still
I juxtapose the camera lens, waiting,
Every shot I take changes track
life is ruined beyond all repair, I shimmer
through a maddened dream of swimming
in a strange pool with people I do not wish to
know,
in this very pool with people I call friends
the dogs speak with uncertain hands,
'there is no you, you died a hundred deaths'
in a space with no boundaries or edge
while the moon growls out loud, waning still,
'there are no dead bodies here', BUT
I can smell the cadavers, 'no other truth I sell:
only separation and death'.

Ducks in a row

The night is bored,
the black it wears,
torn at the shoulders...
forever painted bleak,
bringing in the darkness
night after night with no
other colour it ever wore.
The evening listens to the song
of the last koel that called
and went and waited
at the temple steps
crossed legged,
but no one returned at night
to open that door.

The day waits, silent
for the clamour and noise
we humans paint it with
all the reds and yellows
and flowers of gold.
But the day is unhappy,
no one once looks at its soul.
Ask me what I think of,
the darkness of your passing,
the blessing from that temple,

or the colours of the day?
I will laugh in your face
and tell you this much:
all these don't matter anymore.

Restart

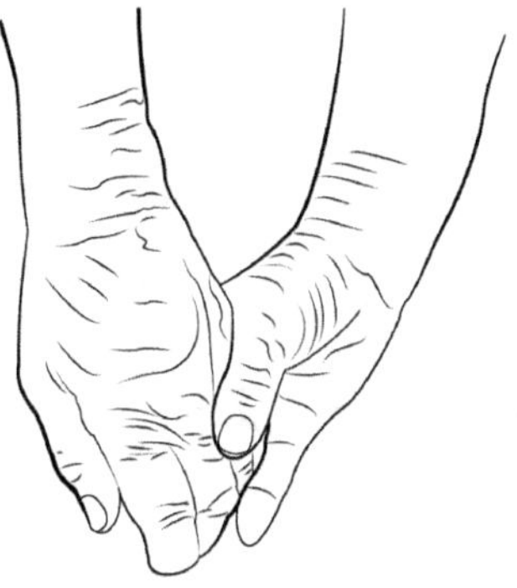

"Time is not linear but a deck of cards that is continuously shuffled." –Paul Tremblay (The Pallbearers Club).

After those long nights
have been stored for another day
and relegated to the back of the closet,
there's nothing to fear,
save that the moon is turning away
and the night will be at its darkest.

But the moon will rise again
and musical laughter will lure you
into play, for as sure as the tides rise and fall
as sure as there is life on Earth,

you will rise again. And I will ride too
upon the light that shines through it all.

And we will laugh and how,
for hospitals teach you patience
and empathy, while super-markets
teach you to be rushed; learn then,
to keep that balance
of both the Master and the Fool.

Time is fickle, time will not wait
forever changing, the deck of cards,
shuffled, re-shuffled changing hands
as you are dealt with a knave, an ace,
did you ever get a full house, a three
of spades? What fun, all cards are one.

Time is the shifting sand on the shore,
the breakers caressing your feet
or shattering to send you tumbling
away into the sand, on your hands and knees
with a mouthful of salt, sand slithering,
the same sand we make castles with.

After these worlds have been folded away
and locked in the library that houses
your thoughts, there's nothing to fear:
you have yourself. You need no one else,

to take you through that board game called 'Life'
that spirited game we have to play, every day.

For nothing that ends is an ending.
It is just a beginning waiting to end
for all beginnings have to stop somewhere,
if you're lucky, on route, you'll find a friend.
I searched for answers but never found them,
only an odd benign refrain, 'begin again'.

Burned

I want to write life and living
in different measurements.
An inch of blood, a spool of grief,
a whit of joy or unhappiness,
a quarter of the sand of the past,
the salinity of impermanence.

That night I tossed and turned
awash in seas of despair...
From far, far (too far, I thought)
a well-known voice returned to repair
my wounded days, endless nights
and said, *Life never promised 'fair,'*

it's only those who have too much
who think they have nothing
it's only those who work on who they are...
who can hold on to something.
Even if the world breaks down
because YOU think it's 'unfair'

Only the tough survive,
only because they care.
You cannot play with knives,
and not expect a scar;

You cannot live with dogs
and not live with fur;
You cannot learn to cook
and expect never to be burned...
and you can never, never love someone
and expect it returned!

The body

The body lies on a steel table
All around it, people stand
Scrubbing, cleaning, harvesting
As in fruits from an orchard.

Embalmed and disarmed
I see you as you saunter off
Your hands in your pockets
Whistling a familiar chord

I know the smell of death, I think,
That stench of rot
And formaldehyde
That refuses to wash off.

Words I thought I never would hear,
Spoken to cleave the soul
The cadaver floats away
In a sea of faces long gone.

'This is how it is,' you smile
Refusing to acknowledge my pain,
'This is the way of the world, see?
All of life is an illusion, your cares in vain.'

Are these, then illusions too?
Those hands I hold in mine?
Your voice calling to me in the dark
Across gurneys abandoned by time?

My hands now man the oars
'A little to the left,' you used to say
'both hands must pull together
If you want to go straight.'

So am I going straight?
My hands have unequal power
Water leaks from eyes
That told you I would never cry.

But cry I did. Like a child,
Like a man whose roof is snatched
In the middle of a storm.

I stand where I always stood.

Here in this room
Naked in my aloneness
With you in my head for company
And the dead body I visit again and again.

In the cold hospital room
Where time stands still.
And I wait for you to speak.
To my restless soul.

In the graveyard

In this graveyard, a boy once proposed to me,
We were young and callous and the world
Lay at our feet. We climbed the broken wall
To get inside, we did that often, my friends and I
Daring each other to stay on till dark, exploring
Among tombstones, reading aloud the words
Left for the dead. So when this bright-eyed boy
Actually held out a ring, it felt a little strange
But not really, because those days doing things
That others thought strange was ordinary.
I was in control of my life, Of course, I broke
The boy's heart, maybe for a little while.

In that very graveyard where some ancestors
Lie buried, we used to sit on tombstones
And tell each other stories and dream
Of futures yet to unfold. When I returned
A few days ago, the sunlight fell differently
The light had changed. The years had left
Their mark, both on me and the graves.
I watched the burial from a little afar.
Saw the kite that hung on the tree above
Helplessly fluttering to be free,
for some force of nature to cut it loose,
To strike that connecting bit of string.

In that graveyard to which I returned
I left a little of myself that day, not on the earth
But fluttering in the breeze much like the kite
Hanging by a piece of string, the ties that defined
Who I could be. Trying to reinvent myself,
One case at a time, whether I lose or win
One length at a time, even if I fail to swim
one drink at a time that I do not pour,
one risk at a time, unafraid of the sour
taste of failure that I hid from all these years
To free my own soul. Of course, I'll break
Your heart, maybe even for a little while.

The boat

For every silver lining hiding a cloud
can wreck your hearth and home.
For every two birds your eyes will see
one or the other will have flown.

For every light at the end of a tunnel
is a train to mow you down.
For every pretty fish in the sea
there is a shark lurking around.

For every blessing in disguise,
for every finger crossed in hope
there's always a heavy price to pay,
no time to regret or to mope.

So set your sails on your own terms
the waters are dark and bloodied
carrying voices of the dead children
and the ones I never carried.

Cross that river, find the other side...
there's always more than you'll ever know
and lest you falter, lest you deride
I am on that bloody boat, waiting to row.

I do not lead

In a life I do not lead, I sit in a cell
cold and harsh and flooded with light
imagining how your hands
held mine
and led me through frosted fields
bathed in moonshine.

In a life I do not lead, I still am walking
upon those star-lit nights
loud as the ghosts that walked
by our side,
silent as the graves and the voices
rising in the night.

In a life I do not lead, I do not pick
at my scars, your fingers trace
the bleeding scabs, healing each
and everyone,
I am that wound calling out to you,
begging to return.

In a life I do not lead, I am that book
you pick up and smile as you read
leafing through the pages of hurt, you know
you're here for me

even as morning comes and we agree
that we disagree.

Erasing Bodies

After the dead have been put away,
their bodies lie as shells on a beach,
the limbs that danced with life
shut down forever, waiting to be picked up,
cremated, donated, buried or thrown
for vultures to feast.

                      I call
upon the bodies I own, my past loves
my mistakes, even that drunken phone
in the dead of night. Does anybody know
where the dead go? I think they wait,
sometimes quietly, make their presence known
they live in our bones,

                      sometimes chill
our souls, burning into a memory
as the real bodies pile up, like my father's
which never left me, although
I watched him burn, brought back the ashes
And floated them away, I turn
to him, 'there is a crisis',

                      I say,
'We have to erase the bodies

that eat away at bone and flesh,
maybe a mass grave is best,
quicklime will do the trick, I heard!'
His laughter echoes in my ears:
'Yes, but will that erase your heart?'

Unbeaten

I have learned to live with Ghosts
they often break bread with me, they
taught me to run headlong into the Storm,
stride out into the Darkness,
for waiting for the Rain to stop
never would help me... or anyone.

I have had plenty lessons along the way
on how to be Lightning, scorching
the earth below, burning bridges
on my path. I was born to suck the marrow
out of life, to ride shotgun
in coaches with tone-deaf judges.

I have learned to birth fires within
my soul, lying awake to sprint
and Fight in defense of my children
and their children's children,
I have drowned in Longing
but learned to swim in silence.

I am the Subpoenas that make
hard men stutter as they wait their turn,
I am Impatience and Fury, rolled into one
I can wait, as meek as a kitten

as anxious as an owl in daylight
as mad as a dog who has bitten.

So do not come to me with your Lies,
do not ask for Trust once it's been broken
for I have met my share of Hurt and Dismay
who have taught me only to be Strong,
to dare anything and everything
and to call out the apple that is rotten.

My mother tried. She tried to teach
me Manners and things that do not matter
but on the night Thunder shattered,
I learned to chase the Tornado.
To run as far as I can run, to be
more than I can ever be, even Battered.

I have chased the clouds ever since
and the moon, (never forget the moon)
committed myself to Fight not Flight
never mapping myself as unlovable
and never afraid of the shell I was,
where Pain gathers, I carry on.

Home

I have no idea where the days
are slipping, when it is night;
the diurnal circuit fulfilling itself
and time is just a tide.
My time is watching little faces

as they speak and move
the human circuit grinding along
where words have no refuge.
Am I home, I ask myself
is this, then, where I want to be?
Your voice replies: 'home is never a place,
simply a state of being.'
I am home in a hospital bed
I am home when you're with me
I have been freed from spaces
I have come home to be with me.

Where then, do I hang my heart,
the one I gave to you to keep?
And when the rictus circuit closes,
where then, shall I sleep?

Tomorrow

You smell the same, a combination
of Old Spice and talcum powder,
the fragrance I know but never remember,
weaving into my thoughts as I ponder...

Like the letters I wrote but never posted
the letters that returned 'Address unknown',
I am that person, that unknown girl
that I already have grieved but walks alone.

Yes, she crawls through the window
on long dark nights, her face
is the face I see, the one I buried
and burned. I have no answers for her.

I mourn you just as you did when you left,
but no one is gone forever. Forever
is a dirty word, clingy, hapless, I'd rather
you give me 'tomorrow', let me know how to live.

Let me know how the beasts lived up,
how you let them set themselves free...
To live without a care, to let that feeling go
to tell that child at the window, she is home.

Our worlds

We turned midnight into dawn
out of ceilings carved with music
we made atriums
out of our souls, setting them alight
in crystal wind-chimes
hung them from rooftops
so they appeared to float mid-air.

We turned baby teeth into bracelets
wore the Milky Way on our wrists
and the planets danced just for us
our bodies changing
into birds that flew home at sunset,
our breath created vapours
that fed the seas, till the tsunami of our thoughts
let the dams overflow
and set the marine life free
we sat in silence in the forest
our bodies rooting into the ground
to heal the core of the earth,
the wild orchids and us.

The right side of our brain
aligned with the other and we hung
our thoughts out to dry

on the washing line,
when the wind whipped up a gale
we believed that the sunlight
would keep our dreams safely tucked away,
we knew ourselves as well as we knew
each other, we did not need a mirror
to see what we reflected.

Even the seas rushed into our arms
the deserts cut into our bones
and we walked like queens
upon these beaches
sinking our toes in the sand,
bleached by the sun in our hands,
there was much eloquence
and we were unafraid
of the demons and djinns
that were hounded upon us.

There was also peace
and we were certain
we would win
this time around,
BUT there was a world
there was a whole world
we failed to conquer.
And we live it now.

Afloat

We indulge our passions, unthinking
of the ripples we make. I am most alive
when I am dead underwater, cocooned
in its gentle caress. No hacking cough,
not even the pain that shoots
down my leg on land.
This poem flows therefrom
like the drops that slide off my back
as I take a turn and swim away,
my father was right, I was born not to sink
but to swim on a cold dawn when the moon
waxing gibbous sought me out
from hiding and told me to float
float away, stay afloat,
and that is where you will find me,
my past a shroud across my shoulders,
naked, tender and weightless,
staying afloat.

Different Shores

All seas are one, in a manner of speaking,
water flows to water. Standing in the Bay of
Bengal
my feet are touched by waves that may have kissed
Pacific shores. No matter how we look at it,
all Gods too, are one, even the ones that are not.

I thought of my mother, on a Fowler's bed,
who could not feel the sea breeze again.
And I thought of my long-dead father, who told
me
never to hold back, to squeeze every last drop
out of life, to laugh and love, with abandon.

There was a time I believed that I should stop
doing all the things my father loved, but then
I'd have to stop living. So as long as I am
in this world, I do everything he loved
and I know, in my bones, he lives through me.

So? Does my mother feel the breeze I sit in, does
it
caress her face, can she taste the salt in my mouth
from the surf that sent me tumbling away?
Thoughts tumble into thoughts, thoughts of all
the lives I carry, the bodies that dwell with me.

Condemn me all you want but there are many
routes
that lead to the same corner, many ways to the
same sum,
totals totalling themselves to different answers,
all of which are right. Like the seas of people
touched
by the same waters, kissing different shores.

Last rites

My fathers and I sit by the *Hoogly*.
Lit by diyas glowing on dinghies,
the bustling city with its pancaked lights
refract the water in the fractured night.

They tell me how nice it was to meet
yet another uncle who died last week,
how his son was overtly devotional
the words he spoke at the funeral,

his voice thick with emotion, his stories
jostling with regret, tears and worries,
the skies now have faded into a grey fog
stars vainly try to shine in the smog

that pretends to be a cloud. How
can I explain, that my fathers are now
here with me. I know what they insist
I do and don't. I could happily list

the disapprovals, acceptance, delight
if only I could have some more 'last rites',
I would not sit silently among white-clad
mourners
who pretend to care. I would talk loud and clear

I would tell the world of nights like these
of adventures shared over seven seas
and I'd never regret. Only look back with pride,
to have known these lives. To call them mine.

Building Bridges

Death, when it finally came, had a lover's touch,
stealing into the night
by the glow of candles. I wander in and out, the
guest room bleakly staring at me
waiting for its occupant to return. This is the
everyday as we know it: Spring
is here, and soon the summer heat will pour
through windows.
I check my phone as I wait in queue, this is what
the living do, we wait.
Waiting for the lights to change, to buy a loaf of
bread, for someone to come home.
That day while walking I tripped, that is life, I
thought, you fall and get back up,
trying to walk straight again; we want someone to
talk to, doing something
that would give some joy to our lives. You called it
schadenfreude, what

you finally gave up on. Like the cart of groceries
we left at the checkout,
not bothering to look back or worry about the
bag breaking as we ran
to the car, giggling at our foolishness; I remember
building bridges.
Between your house and mine, and I look back at
ourselves,
staring up at the stars, laughing as we dug into
karela wheels,
sharing that last drink, whose turn was it, to buy
the Rum? I am still
living, that is what the living do. They remember,
and they wait.

The Shroud

I wrote
myself a song
I wove myself a cloth
warm and soft, made of compromise
and lies.

I'll howl
at your grave when the moon is full
I'll drape the shroud 'round me

and dance with you
once more.

Fallen Leaves

My life lies scattered about
like fallen autumn leaves
harried and harassed,
I look about me.

The button I forgot
to sew back on,
that school skirt that is to be hemmed
because it is too long.

The draft that awaits correction
the piled files to be read,
the chicken sweats in the kitchen
waiting to be sautéed!

The homework that's been saved for me,
the sums yet to be done,
the school project screams
for my attention!

Add to this the poem
that's rattling in my head
the savage hunger of my writing
demanding to be fed.

The phone pings a message
emails are always 'urgent'
I set about with a resolve
to bring order to the moment.

I gather up the tasks
list them in my head
I prioritise my work
fit the shopping in as well.

I'm efficient and ruthless
in my will to succeed,
in disposing of my chores
yes, I have so decreed!

Then I happen to glance
out the open window,
where mauve clouds dance

in golden egg-yolk yellow.

The sky is washed in pink
and grey streaked with night,
a gush, a hint of rain
and I am lost in its light.

The window rattles in
a rush of fresh breeze
and my lists are scattered again
like fallen autumn leaves...

Drudgery

That night I looked up at the sky
where the half-moon hung; its glow
a tarnished lantern billowing up high
all alone. 'Help me', I choked and said,
'I'm tired, my bones ache, the drudgery
of housework is beginning to take
its toll; my hands are heavy, I feel their weight
this life has passed its "sell-by" date'.

In my dream my father stood, silent and still,
a familiar half smile playing on his lips
his eyes glittered with tears, or was it glee?
And in the semi-darkness I heard him speak:
'I'm there with you, I hear every sigh
I'm certain I taught you better than to cry,
hard work surely cannot defeat you
expiry dates are luxuries for the weak.'

'But I am tired, this body is frail
the spirit is weak, I know I cannot face
the thought of living like this for another day
surely I cannot do this', I whine in pain.
'Look around you, you are blessed
you have your own hands, legs that bear your
weight

there are many who have less, but carry on
nevertheless. Frailty is only a mental game.'

I woke, the tears wet on my face, I wished
I could hold on to the image, that passing glow
and then realised, I do. In each arm that lifts,
in every breath, in every smile, in each refrain.
Work and routine, all come to pass,
it's the spirit that remains, the soul goes last,
and my soul walks with one of the best,
his strength, his laughter in my veins.

Always and forever (A sestina)

'The dead have a tendency to stay dead,'
wasn't that what you said, with that sad smile?
I remember that day clearly, those grey clouds
threatening to burst through my innocence,
my tiny voice asking if it meant forever
as the cadaver burned in orange flames.

My eyes see past those long-dead flames
among multitudes who have stayed dead,
they have been etched in my heart forever,
along with the lesson you gave with that soft smile
muting the voices of shameful innocence,
my protests hanging like ominous clouds.

Your memories trail like bright clouds,
hanging over my head in sunsets of flame,
where pink flowers dance to songs of innocents
murdered under heavy feet, now very dead.
In this decay, only thoughts of you make me
smile...
I stop to think that in this life there is no forever.

It is a trite word, that one: the pompous 'forever'

for everything evaporates in cottony clouds
even when I think I remember your smile
It's taken from a picture in fading shades and
flames.
And a day will come, I know. I will die. And stay
dead.
And your memories will die along with my
innocence.

Yes, my crime is my unwavering innocence,
imagining that anything I do will last forever,
penning thoughts to paper, words brittle and
dead,
as they hit the website in digital translucent
clouds
clouds that rise and shine to go out in flames
shimmering into nothing in the light of day: like
your smile.

There's nothing I yearn to see more than your
smile
and relive those childhood days of innocence,
those seashells we picked speckled with purple
flames,
pretending we could hear the ocean forever...
under skies littered with puppy-like clouds
running carefree and happy in days long dead.

I continue to live and smile though I know you are dead, my unworthy innocence murdered in ominous clouds, the simmering flames tell me you're here. Always and forever.

Broken Sky

There's a hole in the roof where the storm came
through
at night when it poured and the wind blew
in gales, uprooting trees, followed by thunder
lightning striking, my fears asunder.
I must have blacked out... for when I woke up
the sky was smiling sweetly and was blue
I waited, I waited for three days or was it more?

I called for you, Ma, I knew you were home.
but you did not answer; I thought of the game
of hide and seek we used to play
expecting you to jump out at me
with a smile on your face. And a *nimki*
in your hand, and you'd sling
my worthless limbs over your shoulder,
and together we would watch the sun

as it set over the mangroves, and you'd point
out the stars one by one and tell me stories
of each, and not let me see the tear
you hid in the corner of your saree...

Have you had enough of me, Ma?
This child of yours, unable to uproot
herself from earth?
Have you given up on me?
I waited but you did not come Ma, so I tried
I tried to get out of my bed
but fell down instead.

So I dragged myself to the other side,
only to find you lying here, your body stiff
and cold but the sari, still damp
as if all the tears you hid and cried
since I was born were buried inside
Will they take me away, Ma, if they know
send me to the father whose hands
you saved me from when you said, 'let's go'?

Surely you know I cannot return.
So I rest my head upon your breast, Ma,
I am not hungry anymore.
The world can wait, I wait here with you, Ma,
and gaze upon our piece of broken sky
as it filters into our home.

We are safe (Cyclone Amphan)

The rain lashed the walls of my face,
each drop piercing the skin as I chased
the old unused tent that threatened to fly
off the terrace. Someone gave that tent
to my daughters for them to play with,
and there it stayed for years thereafter, out-grown,
but not remembered to be thrown.
The clouds raced their chariots across the sky
in gun-metal grey and charcoal, as birds
flapped their wings against the breeze, searching
for a way out of the storm, a place to call home
even for a while. The wind blew in a flower
from three houses down. The maid silently weeps
as her daughter cannot be reached,

she did not go to the evacuation centre
and the embankments have been breached.
But we are safe here, in our homes.

Outside the cyclone rages, winds blowing
every which way, nature is so fierce, someone
wails,
nature reminds us, now and again, how small,

how helpless we all are. How small and useless,
how weak and ineffective are our mighty towers.
Aluminium sheets from that fancy building
rained from the sky, others danced the streets
turning jagged corners as the wind
spun them in the air. Trees have fallen
as trees in concrete tend to, their roots
not deep enough to withstand a storm.
The wind blew in a flower from three houses
down. How strong are the roots that you cling to?
Where do you go when you want to be home? Can
you endure this destruction? Do you have yourself
to hang onto? Do you seek or do you provide
shelter in a storm? I ask, for we are safe here, in
our homes.

There is a mother unable to feed her child
who feeds her hunger with drain water tonight
A father who carries the world on shoulders
that never have shuddered in delight.
Then, of course, there is Facebook,
asking, are you safe in the cyclone?
Have you kept your distance, have you been
spared,
the whimsical vagaries of nature, are you home?
How are they, those who were walking?
Those whose homes have been washed away?
The wind had no sense of direction, it blew

in a flower from three houses down.
But where does the blood and water flow?
These are things we only debate and discuss
talking in hushed voices, watching, wide-eyed
in videos forwarded in clusters of shame.
You see, we are safe. In our homes.

Abandoned

I found a little boy on the swing set
when I took the dogs out before dawn.
His face was streaked with tears
in his hands, he clutched a cloth
with which he tried to cover his face
fear upon his visage wrought.
I almost voiced the obvious question,
'How did you get here'? Something
stopped me, I looked at him, almost
translucent in the receding night,
fat tears rolled down his face,
I almost missed his whispered plea,
'I want my mother, where is my mother?
She did not wake after she lay to sleep,
She said she would come back for me!'
'Where do you stay'? I asked, distraught
full of anguish and disbelief
'Everywhere,' he said quietly, 'in places you do not
see.
Don't leave me stranded, take me home, please.'
While I was pondering the logistics
of how and who and what and when
the chance to save him slipped away,

for he was gone when I looked again.

I went back to bed, sleeplessly tossed,
convinced myself it was just a dream.

I found him in the morning news.
pawing at the blanket of a dead mother
brooding black eyes looking straight at me.

Mass Cremation

I want to steal some lives
from the pyres around me
steal some smiles from those
who died breathlessly
reaching out and finding
no hands pressed in return
and I want to hear their stories
yes, each and every one.
And scream their joys
from the mountains
so the world will not forget
the weight of their burden.

Illumination

That small city lulled my senses
each evening's walk in the large renowned park
winding between old trees and curated lawns.
Do you know, they are setting up lights?
To make it look like a fairyland
or another ostentatious Indian wedding,
I won't be here. And not a minute too soon.
For as I went for my walk today,
the park was closed. I took the long road home
they're illuminating the park, the guard said,
smiling, 'No visitors today.'
Someone grabbed my breast.
He came from behind on a bike
had the cheek to smile as he looked back

'Bastard' I yelled, violated. Picked up a brick
but he was gone. At the corner, a man looked up
asked me what was wrong. A guard came out of a
house.
Some uniformed men watched, I ran
back home, the stone still in hand.
They're setting up lights, it is announced.
Talking to my daughter,
who knew not what hit her.
Why, then, do we walk in darkness?
It was full light, only 4:30 pm. Do they even know
what dark looks like? I wasn't showing any flesh
I wasn't even asking for it. It was just a walk
in broad daylight. Do they know what darkness is?

Dark is a woman of fifty
being pawed by a man
just because he can.
Dark is the colour of lies
told to appease in twilight,
Yes, they will set up lights. But
lights are the women who dare
every day. To be out there...
Lights are the women who silently fight. Every
day.
Who are 'they', then, to illuminate lights?

Corpses

We are all dying here, some slower than others
the corpses that matter are calling out to us,
that phone you bought will not reach the network
where the corpses that matter are claiming us.
The man crossing the road out of sight, crosses
not knowing how far is too far, how far will we all
return? For the corpses that matter
are watching, the pomp and splendour that you
cling to will fall away like dead skin clinging to
the soul.
And you will stand naked, for the corpses that
matter will certainly return. To take us home.

Death toll

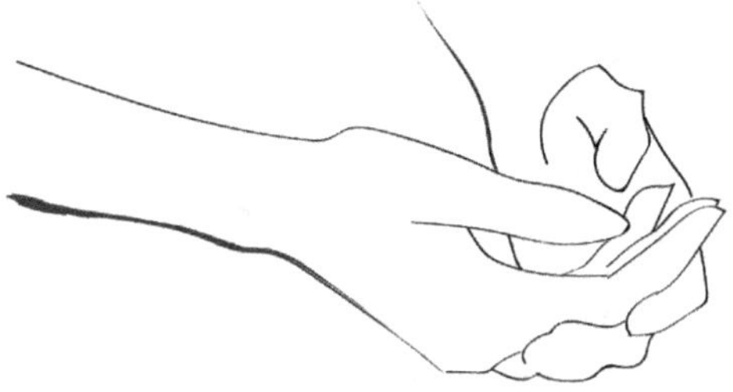

There are no opioids here,
no wisdom to be shared.
The bitterness of the pill
is directly proportional
to your love for everything
human. Which is not always
lovable. Yet there are people
who hold our hearts
those that we think of and
wish to keep safe.
Alas, the COVID has no country
or calling. It moves among us
as with those we love.
How can you 'be safe'?

What is safety, then,
protection for the privileged few

you have allowed in your life?
And a sense of relief
when you see the dead
are not yours?
But they are gasping for breath,
dying in droves out there,
the unknowns,
also someone's mother, son
father, daughter, wife?
I flounder and flail,
while you argue conspiracy theories
and rail. Against the dying of a sun.
Do not look to me for comfort,
Let this poem be the one.

Peace at last

It poured that evening after that crematorium,
the man there collecting the dead like piles of
leaves,
leaves that have fallen from trees bursting with
summer
while the garden lies untended, with no one to
stop
and admire the flowers that were your joy and
pride.

The skies darkened to black and rain lashed the
streets
streets that you once walked, we watched from
our room
as the wind blew away all that was old and rotten,
dust swirling to settle into a sweet cool breeze.
I wonder if you felt it too, or was that just salt on
my lips...

The tears, the tears came later, the darkness
pressing into me
like an unwelcome lover. Others lurk in the
unblinking darkness
figures, shadows hiding within shadows. For the
dead never leave us,

I shall carry you inside me, another body to add
to my growing collection.
I think of you often, something beautiful that
cannot be recreated
without being ruined. I ruminate, picturing you as
you raise your club
to hit that perfect swing, laughter twinkling in
your eyes, limbs surging with life
raising a toast in a place filled with happy
shadows, peace at last.

Dirge to humanity

He raped a three-year-old.
Yes, in a stationary bus.
While her five-year-old brother
screamed to let her go, alas!
It did not make the front pages,
a rag-picker's child rarely does.
Some read the news and shuddered,
'Thank God it's not us.'
And some saw it and said,
'Say a Muslim did it, not us!'
The children got lost in the telling,
too few felt the thrust
of the knife in humanity
as it fell, oozing blood and pus.
The last shreds of conscience
sad clowns in a circus,
Thank God, it's not us.
'Thank God, it's not us!'

Just because I am quiet

My father was forged with fire,
if he saw injustice, he fought it through
he walked on burning coals and argued for causes
by the time it was passed to me, the fire had
quietened.
I do not rage against dark nights
my nature is more amenable, even selfish,
I like to stay out of fights
to each his own, live and let live.
But let that not blind you
to the darkened rage that burns
when I read about the girls
touched and cast aside like rag dolls
when day after day after day
young and old women are raped
when I listen to the wimps in denial
twisting words, playing the same blame games.
I can remember too easily the safety pin
that I used on crowded buses, the duck walk on
the streets
they did not keep me unmolested
nothing kept us safe from those prying hands
prying hands that made us feel dirty
prying hands that disappeared in the crowd
even as we stood stunned into shame and silence

and brothers, fathers asked us what was wrong.
I too am afraid, I too rage, my blood boils
my heartbeat threatens to burst from my veins
and shatter into a million pieces
as I wait, wait for a chance to be the change
to bear the torch, to carry the flame
to somehow protect these women, these girls,
these children

our daughters, our nieces, our friends
our own selves from these vile hands and minds.
Do not make the mistake of judging me
or think that I am weak
Do not once think I will not fight back
or that you have my consent.
For the blood that flows in me was forged of fire
and a single spark can bring down forests
lay waste to your sterile house and gardens.
Do not think I will sit quietly just because I am quiet.

The corner of your eye

When I am gone
forget my unruly hair
the vague, vacant stare
when I knew not what you said
Forget then the fights we had
unless some make you smile
forget my weak efforts at style
and all the faux pas I made

When I am gone
find that photo from the album
yes, that one: head up, smiling
keep that one nearby.
Remember how my eyes light up
when I see you today
remember your hands that under
the pillow to mine stray

When I am gone
hate me for leaving,
but remember the dreams
that we share, don't let them die
Believe in us like we do today
Live, without goodbyes
and I will be with you always...
hidden. In the corner of your eye.

Eight

In my mind I am an octopus, the colours of my
body changing as I sleep; the yellows of
contentment, the greys of the bleak worries, dyed
in bleach. The deep blue shades of peaceful
slumber, the frowning blacks as I refrain from
speech.
I do not speak to the dead anymore
I do not tell them to meet you, for they are gone
the ones you knew, the ones I love enough
for you to know. I only watch from afar
ragged breaths lost mid-air, browned, rough.
Eight are the arms of the warrior goddess,
Eight are the paths, I hum to myself.
Thoughts unravel as I pick up the threads
where they wind, sometimes entwined
into eight tentacles of words left unsaid.

In the end, it is easy to turn away, in the end
the purest smell is not of incense but the mixture
of wood and flesh burning, scraps of ash taking
wing.
I gaze beyond dark clouds that threaten to burst
And ask myself, how long is a piece of string?

From a crematorium

You see a dirty floor
I see a vulnerable
young girl
cradling the head
of her dead father
unable to look at me
with dead-pan eyes
or even cry.

She tries to find solace
in the Gita
someone thrust
into her hands
the words swim
as, wide-eyed, she reads:
'Thou grievest
where no grief should be'.

I want to reach out
to that girl
from long ago
the one whose heart
is breaking
the one who's wearing
her grief
like a new cloak.

I want to tell her
that she will return
to this spot again and again
and it will be alright
to grieve
and that cloak she will always wear
from long ago
will be made of the purest light.

Full moon again

Through the open window
moonlight shimmers on the floor
the sharp rain has rinsed clean
the yellowed stains of the day.
Only your thumbprint remains
etched into the skin below my ear
where you touched me that last time
before you went away.

The moon marches in swathes of light
as I lie awake, sensing, not seeing
its journey across the sky
corseted in shadows of clouds and lace.
Sounds of life are muted
by the chatter of my pen on paper
you watch me frown over my whys
denying – that we share this space.

For full moons bring memories
in smoke and winter fires
your voice a burst of cold air
that washes over my deepest nights.
I look up from the page
certain I will see you here:
all my thoughts, naked and raw,
startled, like birds, into flight

Zephyr

When I die, scatter my ashes
Somewhere like this.
Where the morning creeps in
On the wings of a whistling
Thrush. Where nightjars
Ballet with the call of the frog
Where the mist lifts
Long after the day has dawned.
Where blue hills stretch away
As far as eyes can see. There,
let me be blown in the wind.
And should you ever feel the need to visit
Go somewhere no one can reach you
And call my name. I won't be there.
But it will feel as though I am.

Phanush (sky lantern)

If I walked to the ledge where the sun sets,
would I fall off the edge of the Earth?
Or are my words mere mechanical toys
on which you build home and hearth?
I had a dream once but it shattered,
left me clawing at the one who gave me birth.
Now I try to fill shoes that were left empty
Ill-equipped to prove or deny my worth.

What is worth if it requires proving,
tumbled thoughts gone in the blink of an eye
Where do you go when you need soothing?
Where do the tears go that we do not cry?
If you ask me, silence is the best seasoning
one day all your noise and spitfire will die.

One day I too will go out quietly blazing,
A lone phanush in your smoke-filled sky.

Adding Up

‘I am walking at a speed of 4.5 miles an hour.
You start after ten minutes and walk
At a speed of 7.24 km. How long will it take
For you to overtake me?’ Those sums
were your favourites. Along with the tank
that rarely got filled, and sometimes
overflowed. How I feared that morning ritual,
waiting for you to give me problems to solve.
Math was everything, you said.
I dared not argue, quietly adding numbers
till I gave up. I tried to pass on
your love for numbers but failed.

Not everything in life adds up,
not every x has a solution, sometimes integers
need to be expressed in decimals.
I still tried. To live life by your rules
to play the game in hexagonal bubbles
to live within concentric circles,
but nothing adds up. If there is one thing
I learnt, it's that there are no whole numbers
in Life. Like that tank that never gets filled,
there is a tap to bleed it dry. And how much?
How much further must I walk?
Till I finally catch up with you?

Timeline photos

Scrolling through timelines
I realise how we mentally compartmentalise
events in our heads. Look at these pictures...
that was the last dinner we went to together,
here is the wedding the year Ma died.
See, those are of the first vacation without her,
this was the last holiday with Baba. It's funny
how the person in the pictures disappear
only to reappear in memories,
in photos dragged out of old albums
and shared again and again,
somehow bringing to life a void
that never is not emptied, an abyss
holding an image of happier times,
of a deepening darkness as we look inside
and cannot find the people we seek.
I feel the weight of that nothingness
that clinging fragrance, that voice I heard
only a while ago. Has it really been that long?
If only pictures could speak and memories be
erased
as quietly as the people who touch our lives are
gone
banished from our ever-afters. Forever.

Cutting corners

I keep seeing you, in the unlikeliest places
certain that you were in that corner
last night under the street lamp
the scratch of a match as you lit your pipe.
And there by the lake, striding
in front of me, just out of earshot
I run to catch up, my legs turning to lead
as you turn the corner out of sight.
And often when the thunder rolls
the dogs whine, their ears pinned back
I talk to them softly in a sotto voice,
finding comfort in words we left unsaid.
You don't say much, you don't need to
your baritone resonates in my head.
Cutting corners, taking turns
I cannot let you remain dead

Unearthed

When my soul needs healing
I come to you
Cutting through flesh and tissue
With an expert scalpel
Setting the maggots free
Tearing the skin
Unearthing (in)human remains
A bit of nail, some blood
Some muscle, tissue?
And when it's done
I draw the curtain
Veil the wounds with the usual warts
And hide.
In full view.

The best lines

The best lines are all taken,
so I make do with the ones left behind
re-inventing myself out of rejects,
living my life kicking at daylight
till darkness bleeds in.

I thought I lost the thread of that story,
so I searched for it, crawling on all fours
looking underneath unmade beds
peering over edges and corners
unexplored by the broom.

What is that you carry in your mouth?
It smells of death, the poison seeping
into my clothes, like cigarette smoke
curling from fingers that lean
casually against mine, not quite touching.

Like our lives: lived together but more apart
than as one. Is this how it ends then? In tangled
threads? Will we walk each other?
Matching our footsteps as the tide carries us,
pulling on leashes we cannot see.

While all along the journey,
it is clear that the places I want to go to
are all behind me. You see, all along,
I have been calling out directions
holding the map upside down.

I should have told you

I should have told you
That afterwards I lay my head
On my father's chest and listened
For a beat, some sign that his heart
Remembered. But all I heard
Was the vacuous sound of silence
Calling out my name
In a voice that was no more.

I should have told you
That when my father died
He did not go to any heaven
He still walks in parallel worlds
Waiting to take me home
And it is not because he cannot leave
It is because I will not let him go.

I should have told you
That anyone can be broken
That when lightning strikes a tree
It falls as it stands, the man taking shelter
Glad that he crossed to the other side
I had no such luck, my trees fell
On top of me, leaving me suddenly
Alone, bereft of shade or sanctuary.

I should have told you
That when stars fall, they fall
All the way, blazing through the sky
Even during the day.
But day is night somewhere
The diurnal circuit does not stop.
It does not care about our feelings
Nor does it go away.

I should have told you
That love is sometimes painful and it hurts
Love is a waiting room without an exit
Waiting to see if you like it
Waiting to be, waiting to want
Is there ever enough or not?
Love is hungrily recalibrating
Waiting to be nurtured and fed.

I should have told you
I am just a woman, I have my faults
Every compliment I ever received
Was just that, a mere sentiment
Well meant, but imposters just the same.
Like abuse and scorn, it washed away
I never filigreed my feelings
For you. I never was a poet.

The quilt

I brought myself a bolt of cloth
made of the gentlest words
wrapped it in folds of warmth
and hemmed the sides with love.
I sewed in some heartaches
and tears to make it strong
and embroidered the length
with kantha stitches of loss

This is the quilt I weave for you
for when the nights are cruel
for the vapid winter mornings
when even the sun seems cold.
This is my lonely gift to you
in brilliant shades of azure
for when you call out in the silence
and I will not be there